KU-323-998

YOU ARE REALLY RICH
YOU JUST DON'T KNOW IT YET

....

STEVE HENRY

INTRODUCTION BY DAVID ALBERTS

Published by Virgin Books 2009
Copyright © The Really Rich Partnership 2009

Photo pp. 14-5, 34, 43, 52, 72-3, 109, 112 © Scott Wishart
Photo pp. 54-5 © 2008 Bernarda Gospic
Photo p. 82 © Paul Taylor
Photo p. 89 (apple) © Dorling Kindersley

First published in Great Britain in 2009 by
Virgin Books
Random House, 20 Vauxhall Bridge Road,
London SW1V 2SA

www.virginbooks.com
www.rbooks.co.uk

Addresses for companies within The Random House Group Limited can be found at:
www.randomhouse.co.uk/offices.htm

The Random House Group Limited Reg. No. 954009

A CIP catalogue record for this book
is available from the British Library

ISBN 9780753519806

Printed and bound in Italy by L.E.G.O S.p.A

CONTENTS

INTRODUCTION

This book is about a new value system.

An alternative to a purely financial system.

Partly because, as a direct result of the credit crunch, people are exploring different ways of living. And they're looking for something to replace money as a general criterion for value.

Because – let's face it – we all bought into it too much.

Oscar Wilde's description of a cynic – someone who knows the price of everything and the value of nothing – was starting to apply to all of us.

We'd all become, in one way or another, hooked on money.

Now, you always get those people who say that it isn't money which is the root of all evil, it's the love of money which is the root of all evil.

But that seems unnecessarily pedantic to us. I mean, we all fell in love with it.

And, as a result of that, we all felt we didn't have enough of it.

In Britain, we got into the Recession before any other country. And we've gone into it deeper than any other country.

So much so, that we got into a "recession obsession". That could be down to the famous British "Blitz spirit". The belief that tightening your belt and having a cold shower is good for you.

But there's another way of looking at it.

Which is to see it as a symptom of British inventiveness and creativity.

The same British spirit which invented everything from the steam train to the internet to punk rock.

Because there's something inside a lot of us that was asking questions about consumerism.

Was two thousand years of civilization really reaching its peak in the belief that you needed to spend £100 on a new iPod because they'd brought one out that was purple?

Or was there actually more to life than this?

There was something inside us which welcomed some aspects of the Recession. "We can't afford a new car this year" – well, good. The old car was working perfectly well, and I'm rather fond of it.

There's something about the British brain that asks – restlessly, relentlessly – what's next? Is there something better than this?

IT'S THE END OF THE WORLD AS WE KNOW IT (AND I FEEL FINE)

We wanted to find out what on earth was really going on?

(Partly because nobody else could tell us, partly because that's what we do.)

So we went out and asked people how happy they were, and what would actually help to make them happier.

And whether it's because they are just sick of watching the pound plummet or whether the penny has actually dropped, to our pleasant surprise, very few mentioned money.

The people we spoke to focused on family occasions, hanging with friends, quiet time on their own, seeing grandchildren, and visiting places they had never seen before as things that made a real difference in their lives.

Moments that they would never trade for anything, experiences that were described as priceless.

And maybe that's the point of the recession.

To make us all stop and think about the value of the things we really value.

To understand that a good weekend could be seen as "worth-more" and the obsessive pursuit of cash as "worth-less".

Whether it is life balance or bank balance, the fact is we need a new currency.

HOW REALLY RICH ARE YOU?

We spoke to 1,000 people and asked them to rate how happy fifty life events and experiences would make them, along with five items of monetary value.

Averaging and comparing these different ratings allowed us to estimate the price of the priceless.

There are fifty topics and, based on our research, we've calculated a monetary value for each one.

Take the time to **Read the book** (according to our calculations you'll be £53,660 richer already) and then simply add up your total in the back of the book.

Good health tops the charts at £180,589, which proves the old adage that 'you can't take it with you' is right.

Having a Child (£123,592) is worth more than **Having a pet**, which is probably a good thing.

Eating Chocolate is worth more than **Looking Good**.

Having Sex (£105,210) on a **Sunny Day** (£89,625) in **The Great Outdoors** (£74,310) whilst on **Holidays** (£91,759) with **Somebody who loves you** (£164,921) is worth a grand total of £525,825.

And if that brings back **Good Memories** to some of you, you've just picked up another (£80,419).

As *The Sunday Times* Rich List celebrates its 21st birthday we thought it would be more in keeping with the times to publish the first Really Rich List.

So when you're finished go to reallyrichlist.com and fill in the survey.

We might just find that there's a baker who is richer than a banker, and a plumber who's really richer than a politician.

And while you're there you might be surprised how Really Rich you really are too.

Enjoy,

David Alberts

Really Rich Multi-millionaire and
Founder of What On Earth Is Going On?

SPENDING TIME WITH FRIENDS

You're never poor if you've got friends.

Because, when the chips are down, you can usually borrow a couple of quid off them.

And, if the price of chips has gone up, you might need to borrow a bit more.

Friends are agreeable things to have. Because they usually agree with you.

For instance, I told my best friend I felt that my whole life had been an empty sham, and he agreed totally.

Of course, some people have got an online profile boasting 18,000 friends – which might suggest that there's some sort of ego problem going on.

So, perhaps we need to define what we mean by a really good friend?

If you say "I've got to get to the airport at 6 am on Friday morning, can you give me a lift?" – a true friend will give you the number of the local cab company before laughing in your face.

Maybe that's what's meant by the phrase "friends are always there for you". Because in most dictionaries, "there" is defined as "somewhere else".

But real friends (as opposed to imaginary friends) are great. They'll back you up and cheer you up, no matter what life throws at you.

A friend indeed is a friend you need.

So what's it worth?
Your pay pal account is worth **£63,256**.

YOU'RE CREATIVE

A lot of people say "I'm not creative" – and deny themselves a whole skip-load of fun.

Maybe they were traumatized when young. Maybe they were trying to make a Christmas decoration out of an old cornflake packet – and then when they put it up, everybody who visited the house laughed themselves stupid at the badly-glued bit of old cock at the top of the Christmas tree.

(Of course, you didn't have to use the Kellogg's logo – but that was probably my biggest mistake.)

But really, the only difference between people who are "creative" and those who aren't, is that the creative ones aren't afraid of failing.

Every creative person has their ups and downs – whether it's Steven Spielberg with *1941* or William Shakespeare with *Timon of Athens*. Creative people know that failure comes with the turf.

But if you do try creating stuff, you'll find almost endless amounts of happiness and fascination waiting for you. There are websites where you can play music even if you're tone deaf. Try doodling using the paintbrush applications on your computer.

Not all art is about chopping a cow in half, sticking it in formaldehyde and calling it "The feeling of loss encountered when one has paid over the odds for half a dead cow".

In fact, very little of it is. And you've got to find your own, unique form of expression.

Antony Gormley used 150 tonnes of weather-resistant steel to make his Angel of the North.

What sort of a Christmas decoration could you make with that?

FORMALDEHYDE

So what's it worth?
This slightly more ethical form of creative accounting increases your riches by **£57,075**.

LIVING IN A PEACEFUL AND SAFE COUNTRY

Go on – give yourself a pat on the back if you haven't declared war on anybody in the last four weeks.

Because war is stressful. As someone said of the First World War – "My dear, the noise. The people."

Or, as John Lennon said – Give Peace a Fucking Chance.

Or was that Bob Geldof? Probably Geldof, he was always using the F word. "Give us your fucking money." "Oy Peaches, fucking come here." "No, it's not fucking convenient for you to read the fucking electricity meter right now."

And I mention Geldof because he was nominated for the Nobel Fucking Peace Prize.

So what's it worth?

There have been countless discussions on the cost of war – what about the price of peace? According to our research, living in a peaceful and safe country is worth **£129,448**.

Fucking twice.

So give yourself some points if you live in a country that's at peace.

If you don't agree with our way of adding up points – well, that may be the problem right there.

Maybe you're like my Grandad who fought against the Germans in 1918, the Fascists in 1937 and the Japanese in 1944.

He couldn't get on with anybody.

TAKING A DAY OFF

If you're stressed – for God's sake, take a break.

Actually, don't worry about God, he's good at taking holidays. I don't just mean the Seventh Day – just look at any calendar and you'll see more religious holidays than any other kind.

You might be forgiven for thinking God was a bit work-shy. If he was around now, he'd probably be living in Spain, talking about running a pub but never quite getting round to it.

And he probably had a hand in that wonderful modern-day concept, the Duvet Day.

For those of you who haven't heard of this, a Duvet Day is where you ring up work and tell your Human Resources person that you want to stay at home that day. Except that, in all probability, they won't be there. Because they take more Duvet Days than anybody else on the planet.

In fact, I think Duvet Days were probably invented by someone in Human Resources called Duvet Dave.

So – take time off from work. Take every day you're allowed. Take some Duvet Days on top of that. If you think you can get away with it, take some Pillow Days, some Bedside Table Days, and some Bathroom Cabinet Days as well.

Of course, there are some people who've been off with stress for the last 4 years. Staying curled up under their duvets, refusing to do anything other than watch Spongebob Squarepants and make small humming noises.

They're the ones who were supposed to be running the banks.

So what's it worth?
£54,428 to put under the mattress if you've taken a Duvet Day lately.

FEEL BETTER,
FEEL FITTER

It is one of the unwritten laws of the universe that doing a bit of exercise will make you feel better.

It is another law of the universe that, about 2 days after joining a gym, you'll put your back out.

And, if through some miracle you avoid that pitfall, you'll either feel guilty about not going or turn into a gym junkie, standing naked in front of a mirror and flexing parts of your body you've only just discovered.

The key thing is to do exercise you like doing.

Riding a bike counts as exercise. Swimming counts. Dancing counts.

Walking from the snug bar to the door for a quick fag outside doesn't.

Nor does pushing your luck, stretching the truth, or running up a tab at Ladbroke's.

To keep it fresh, keep trying new things. Next time you're in the gym, why not join the Pilates class?

All they do is stand around, washing their hands.

It's a doddle.

So what's it worth?
At **£36,970**, this is more than enough to be getting exercised about.

TAKE UP A HOBBY

Why are doctors always asking you what hobbies you have?

I reckon if I went and saw my GP with the symptoms of some life-threatening disease, wondering how long I've got and whether it's worth setting the Sky+ for next week's TV – he'd still ask me if I had any hobbies.

But they do it for a good reason – hobbies make you feel more relaxed.

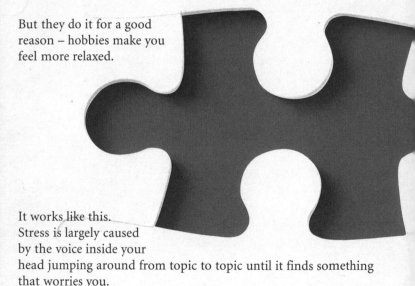

It works like this. Stress is largely caused by the voice inside your head jumping around from topic to topic until it finds something that worries you.

But hobbies make you concentrate on one thing at a time.

It's a bit like meditation in that sense. (Although very few of the top Indian gurus are trainspotters.)

In fact, it's sort of like dynamic meditation, with the benefit of being able to bore other people when you talk about it.

So whether it's glueing bits of plastic together to make replicas of commercial airline fleets, or glueing your holiday souvenirs back together again after you've travelled on some budget commercial airline, keep at it.

The most popular hobby in this country is fishing – the age-old battle between man and denizen of the deep. Although as a friend of mine said, when he saw my catch for that day – "Looks like we're gonna need a smaller bucket".

So what's it worth?
At **£70,041**, that's quite the coin collection you've put together.

CONTEMPLATING BEAUTIFUL THINGS

In that fine film *American Beauty*, the thought is put forward that life is worth living just for the sheer physical beauty all around us.

So, even if you've got a lousy job and your relationship has broken down, it's still worth living to appreciate the beauty all around us every day.

And there's a lot of truth in that.

As John Ruskin wrote – the most beautiful things are often the most useless, like peacocks and lilies. Although if I was a peacock, I'd probably be a bit offended by that remark. Especially if I was peacock who'd just been making himself useful around the place.

But maybe that's the point – just to appreciate something, without asking what it's for.

If you open your eyes to appreciate the beauty of – skies, rooftops, the details on a tree, the reflections in a pool of water – you'll be astonished at how good you'll feel.

I've got my own trick for this.

Look at something – and don't allow yourself to use words to describe it. Just appreciate the angles between objects, the depth and texture and colour, and you'll start to understand how painters feel most of the time.

In the film, the guy gets obsessed watching a plastic bag dancing in the wind – so, really, beauty is all around you if you know how to look for it.

So what's it worth?
You might need more than one plastic bag to carry this sum around. Thinking about beauty makes a not unattractive **£41,716**.

And when they find you lurking in the swimming pool changing rooms with a Black and Decker drill, it's the first thing you should say to the arresting officer.

BEING IN THE COUNTRYSIDE

Greenery is better than the folding green stuff, any day of the week.

Nature is just so exquisitely beautiful, it's stunning.

You could spend your entire life just watching a river flow.

And your happiness quotient will go up with virtually every contact you have with Nature.

So, why are there huge numbers of people living in cities and comparatively few people living in the countryside?

We all go chasing – what, exactly? The money, the sex, the nightlife, the shopping?

Well, put it like that…

Or maybe we're just scared that we'll fail the test of "What's that tree called?" These days, only a few major novelists still know the names of trees. And I often think that's why I haven't become a major novelist – I just don't know the difference between a birch and a beech.

Come to that, I'm not 100% sure of the difference between a birch and a bush.

But Nature really is one of the biggies, if we're looking for an alternative value system to money.

You can smell it, touch it, listen to it, look at it – and taste it too, as long as you avoid some of the little red berries.

Not only are there – as everybody knows – an infinite number of snowflakes, with every one different. But every leaf is different. Every blade of grass is different.

That's what Nature is – a never-ending range of different, fascinating patterns.

It's kind of like choosing your curtains at John Lewis – except that the choice is infinite.

So what's it worth?
Where there's muck, there's brass.
£88,077 to be precise.

HAVING SEX

Have you noticed how, in celebrity interviews in newspapers these days, they usually ask them how often they have sex?

Virtually everybody answers – "as often as possible".

And that's all very well as long as it doesn't interfere with basic human actions like breathing, eating, and taking the dog for a walk.

If you find that you're having an orgasm every few minutes whether you're on the bus, in the bakery aisle, or in a Quarterly Projection Meeting with the accounts department, you might be overdoing it.

And there's a new school of thought which says it's more about quality than quantity. Scientists reckon that the woman is much more likely to conceive if the couple are having what one expert called "gourmet sex" – i.e. the sort of sex you have early on in a relationship.

Wild, thrilling, fresh, energetic, intense, mind-blowing sex.

(That's going to be the title of my next book, by the way. Do you think it will sell?)

The key thing to "gourmet sex" is that both partners take time to ensure the other has a satisfying experience. So have a word with your partner – and explain that "gourmet sex" is more than just opening a tin of Bird's custard.

(Although that often works quite well for me.)

So what's it worth?
Our research says if you've enjoyed a bonk lately it is worth **£105,210**. If this leads to a child, see page 86.

THE GREAT OUTDOORS

You don't need to be rich to enjoy fresh air.

But enjoying fresh air will

always make you feel rich.

So what's it worth?
Take a deep breath. This is worth
an extra **£74,310**.

SPENDING TIME
WITH YOUR FAMILY

Blood is thicker than water and some of my relatives are thicker than anyone I've met in any other sphere of life.

And most people feel the same way.

Einstein had a theory of relatives.

$e=mc$ squared.

Where e is Auntie Ethel, who's always been brilliant. But she's balanced by mc, the married cousins, who have always been a pain in the arse.

YOU ARE INVITED
TO READ THE KIDS A STORY
— & —
PUT THEM TO BED

You see, Nature loves to balance things out perfectly and you will have a perfect balance in your relatives between the fantastic "can't live without 'em" brigade and the "I can't believe we share the same genes" bunch.

It helps to explain why Christmas – a time of universal love and goodwill – is also the time when arguments get kicked off that last for 15 years.

So – get together with the good ones. (And quietly and politely drop the others.)

Cherish them as you would a poorly guinea pig which your 3-year-old child was very fond of.

Because the best ones are there for you, through thick and thin.

So what's it worth?
You can wait until a family member dies before you inherit your fortune or you can enjoy every moment with them while they are still here and instantly collect **£110,047**.

KNOWING YOUR NEIGHBOURS

Bad neighbours can make your life a living hell, although it's not always their fault.

Sometimes it can be due to bad floorboards or an unhealthy love for the music of Showadawaddy.

(Sorry about that, Mrs Rafael, by the way. It was just a bad 3 months I was going through.)

There are more disputes about neighbours than virtually anything else. Overhanging apple trees, a shared drive, cooking smells, teenage parties – or just the fact that one day your neighbour unilaterally annexes the Sudetenland.

But.

Imagine if you got to know your neighbours and felt you could pop in for a cup of tea anytime and they would feed the plants and water the cat when you were away.

(I might have got that last bit the wrong way round.)

And then imagine if they're feeling exactly the same way about you…?

So what's it worth?
Love thy neighbour? **At £33,698**, it's got to be worth at least the occasional cup of sugar.

PLAYING TEAM GAMES

In life, women build complex relationships of trust and mutual support with each other (with sometimes just a little smidgeon of competitiveness). Whereas when blokes get together, they kick each other's shins to shreds.

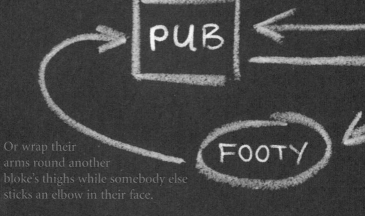

Or wrap their arms round another bloke's thighs while somebody else sticks an elbow in their face.

That said, team games can be a great way to make friends. Whether it's the Rowley Staplers Mixed Rounders Team, the pub footy team, or even the village cricket XI. But be careful when going out to bat for the latter; it's odd how many picturesque country villages suddenly number 6ft 4in West Indians among their residents when the season gets going.

And make sure you don't do that humiliating team-picking thing, one player at a time, where whoever gets picked last feels like killing everybody else in their own team out of sheer spite.

(It's commonly thought that this is what happened to the Manchester United team of 2005, which narrowly failed to win the title. And, to be fair, no top-flight football manager has used the method ever since.)

There are almost endless sports you can get involved in – from korfball to curling.

CURRY

HOME

CLUB

But from where I'm standing, I'd say that Naked Twister is probably the best bet.

Or, more accurately, from where I'm crouching.

So what's it worth?
Have a ball. Make a racket. If you've been partial to a bit of participation recently, you've just netted **£23,475**.

A WALK IN THE PARK

Parks are the only bits of cities where there are no timesheets. They're a gift, on any day of the year.

So stretch your legs. Let the air into your lungs. Raise your chin and point it at the sky.

Watch out for cyclists, flashers, drug addicts, dogs and the odd loony.

Then stride out and feel how good it all feels.

Just don't get carried away. Some of those parks are bigger than they look.

And blisters are God's way of saying that Henry Ford may have had a point.

So what's it worth?
It's not just dog poo you'll be picking up. You've also just scooped a tidy **£47,007**.

REFLECTING ON HAPPY MEMORIES

··

Somebody once said that whoever dies with the most toys, wins.

And somebody else said it's whoever dies with the best memories who wins.

I can't remember who either of those people were, because my memory is terrible these days.

But the second one is right.

And we've all got a memory bank full of lovely memories.

So, enjoy drawing on them. After a certain point, you can live off the interest you've built up over the years.

So what's it worth?
Can you remember the last time you remembered how good those good times really were? If you can, don't forget to add **£80,419** to your balance.

(If you don't have any good memories at all, please contact my publisher. Because they need something new to put in the airport bookshops.)

HAVING TIME TO YOURSELF

**Thomas Hardy could never have written *Far from the Madding Crowd*
if he'd gone down the pub with the madding crowd every night.**

You need time to yourself, for yourself.

Time to potter around, and sort out the sock drawer.

As Pascal said, all mankind's problems could be solved if a person
could just sit alone in a room.

But if you think you'll get bored with your own company after a few
minutes, try the ancient practice of meditation.

If you ever heard the talks given by the Bhagwan Shree Rajneesh, you
would have heard his amazing voice, which was breathy like he was
always on the point of giggling.

That's what meditation can do for you.

Enlightenment can mean lightening up, among other things.

And what helps in meditation is to focus on something.

You can focus on your breathing, or distant sounds, or a simple
phrase. When you do this, you quieten the "monkey brain", which is
otherwise badgering you to buy some milk or get a job as a
shipbroker in Hong Kong.

(That monkey brain is lethal.)

One other tip worth trying is this. The chatter inside your head normally takes the form of phrases that are articulated. Try sl-o-o-o-wing down the chatter. "No-o-o-o mo-o-o-o-o-ney innnnn b-a-a-a-a-a-nk acc-ou-ou-ou-ount."

Believe it or not, just doing that will help.

Then start to sense the quiet and the peace that's always been inside you.

Because, as my brother once said, meditation is a lot better than just sitting around doing nothing.

So what's it worth?
If you have enjoyed a bit of "me time" lately it is worth **£80,558**, but keep it to yourself.

GOING OUT
TO THE FLICKS

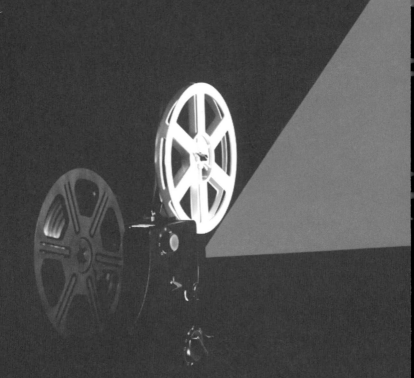

Ask yourself – how many really good evenings have you had at the cinema, versus how many really disappointing ones?

(And sure, there's gonna be the occasional Jean Claude van Damme movie in everybody's life.)

But the cinema is a lovely communal experience, and it's also quite possibly the highest art form of this century.

My tip is to avoid paying the inflated prices at the snack kiosks in cinemas. (And I know that Jean-Luc Godard, the father of the French avant-garde cinema, felt the same way.)

Buy something tasty from a nearby supermarket and sneak it in – they never search you.

Or you could make some nutritious home-made soup at home and well, no – actually, I don't think that'll work.

Just get some nuts and raisins from Tesco.

So what's it worth?
We can't turn you into Slumdog Millionaires on this one. But if you've visited your local lately, the **£21,615** that you collect isn't bad to be getting on with.

PETS

....

Look into those deep brown eyes.

That dog is sitting there thinking – "Is he gonna give me that
chocolate biscuit? That chocolate biscuit I love so much, I love
it more than life itself. If a train came round the corner right
now and headed straight for me, I'd stay here waiting for just
a slim chance of that chocolate biscuit."

And then you eat the whole biscuit.

And they don't hate you.

What kind of love is that?

No wonder we love our pets more than virtually anything else.

Even hamsters have been known to give evidence of
emotional warmth and loyalty.

I had one once who didn't try to escape for a whole day.

So what's it worth?
An additional **£78,640** should have you
purring with pleasure.

SAVOURING THE PEACE AND QUIET

The Quakers believe that you can achieve spiritual balance and happiness through periods of quiet contemplation.

In fact they recommend at least a one-hour session of silence once a week.

What else do we know about the Quakers?

Not much, because they're a quiet, self-effacing bunch.

But apparently they make porridge oats, something that all nutritionists agree is more or less the ideal breakfast.

And they have this thing called "Friends' Houses". And the happiest days of my childhood were spent in friends' houses.

So we might give them the benefit of the doubt on the Quiet Contemplation thought as well.

Give it a try. Just sit in a chair, close your eyes, and feel the quiet.

If you don't believe me, give the Quakers a shout.

So what's it worth?
If this entry wasn't so quiet, we'd say **£89,828** was worth making some noise about.

LISTENING TO MUSIC

We all love music, and with
very good reason. Music can
change your mood faster than almost
anything, and just listening to your
favourite track on a sunny day can seem like
the nearest thing to heaven.

When Sidney Smith was asked for a definition of
Paradise, he replied "Eating paté de foie gras to the
sound of trumpets". And for most of us, our own
personal Nirvana would include a soundtrack by
our own favourite musician.

(And not necessarily Nirvana, unless you're the
type of person with a hank of hair hanging
loosely over half your face like a curtain
that's been hung up all wonky.)

So whatever you're into, get into it. Whether it be Hypno-Trance Borderline Coma Garden Shed, where the crowd in the background chants "You're going home in an ambient", or Electro-Punk-Funk-Drunk-as-a-Skunk George-Formby-on-Acid – if it sounds good, it's doing you good.

Or, to put it more poetically – let the music find the strings inside your soul.

So what's it worth?
An additional **£68,823** from pressing play on the CD player? Sounds good to us.

Quakers believe in the power of quiet.

Wouldn't it be lovely if other faiths were similarly alliteratively motivated?

If the Buddhists believed in bubble baths, the Druids believed in dressing up, and the Christians believed in crispy bacon.

Actually, I think that does cover it for the Druids.

A wise person once said that the best last words you could say would be "Jesus, Allah, Shiva, Buddha – I love you all."

Covering your arse and your options in one short sentence.

However, you don't need to face imminent death to draw satisfaction from faith.

In fact, you don't even need to be religious.

You can draw inspiration from the selflessness you see around you, from the light in a child's eyes when someone helps them, from the warmth and passion and unquenchable love of human charity.

You can draw strength from believing in the power of good to do good.

If you work in one of the well-known trading rooms, don't worry about all this yet.

So what's it worth?
If you believe then we believe you deserve an extra **£36,530**.

DOING THINGS ON THE SPUR OF THE MOMENT

If you've ever gone through that personal hell known as "commuting", you know the deadening effects of habit.

Get on a commuter train and look around you – the people look as though they're being transported to a maximum-security prison in Middle America to share a cell with a man called Ron "Killer Queen" Murano.

Commuting feels terrible because, if you keep doing the same thing over and over again, your spirit rebels.

Your soul, like a baby with a wet nappy, appreciates change.

And spontaneity, while being a tough word to spell, is the answer.

Surprise your partner by kissing them on the nape of the neck, wrapping your arms round their waist and whispering in their ear, "I fancy you like mad, Sweetcheeks." Surprise your work colleagues by making them a cup of coffee. (Don't confuse the two, or you might be in for a bit of a surprise yourself.)

Take the day off work and take the kids to the zoo. The little animals will really appreciate it.

And if you ARE going to share a cell with Ron, and if he drops the soap in the shower, tell him that you had a quick wash that morning in the sink and you're feeling quite clean enough thanks anyway.

So what's it worth?
Don't even think about it, collect **£47,528**
if you've enjoyed some spontaneity.

BEING PART OF THE COMMUNITY

It's all very well talking about communities, and we've all joined Facebook (including my dog who now spends more time online than he does licking his balls, although I sometimes think the two actions are quite similar).

But you'll get a real buzz when you act on behalf of a community. In the real world.

The problem is that most community halls in the UK are about as unattractive an environment as you can get outside of a telephone kiosk with smashed glass in Hull town centre on a wet Monday morning.

So maybe you could just start this off in your own circle of friends.

Why not talk to your newly-befriended neighbours (page 36) about how to make life better in the communal stairwell?

There's nothing inherently wrong with wanting to make the world a better place.

So what's it worth?
All together, that's a community chest of **£33,665**.

A JOB WELL DONE

How's the old mantlepiece looking?

Have you got a prominently displayed invitation from the President of Sarawak to receive an Honorary Doctorate in Humanitarian Studies?

Or just a postcard from Sally that time she went to the Maldives (and sunburnt her arse cheeks so badly)?

Have you got a Bafta for make-up, a worthy reward for all your hard work on "Britain's Ugliest Dog"?

Well of course you haven't, because the person who did that Shitzu's eyelashes, like most of us in most of our jobs, gets no real recognition for it.

But stop for just a second and think of all the good stuff you've done at work.

Make a list of the 10 things you're most proud to have achieved there.

Look at your list, reflect on how damned good you are at your job, and let the feeling of self-satisfaction warm you up like a real fire on a cold day.

So what's it worth?
Job satisfaction offers you a more than satisfactory **£70,676**.

FEELING AT HOME

In the same way that the happiest people aren't usually the richest people, so the nicest homes aren't usually the ones that have had the most money spent on them.

(Did you hear about the party described in one of the gossip mags where the guests were all saying "ouch" a lot, because the host had scattered Swarovski crystals on his deck and it's boat etiquette not to wear shoes on deck? True story. And it proves, yet again, that there is no strict correlation between money and happiness. Or even between money and basic intelligence.)

You've got to spend some money doing your place up, true. But a visit to Ikea, some imagination, some taste, and a sense of fun about the whole thing – that'll give you something far nicer than a £1,000-a-day interior designer pointing at a Vogue spread with impossible white sofas which are just crying out for a dog to get all muddy on them.

Two friends of mine live in a beautiful little apartment, overlooking the rent.

And that's got to be the right attitude.

Home is where we start from. Home is a refuge in difficult times. Home is where we let our friends in, but not our enemies. Home is where you'll always be welcome.

That's got to be worth at least a couple of scatter cushions, hasn't it?

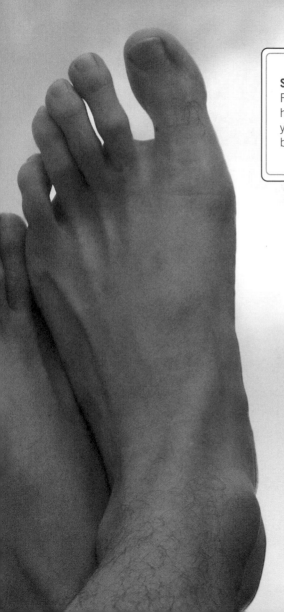

So what's it worth?
Forget about falling house prices – yours has just risen by **£62,693**.

LITERATURE

....

**You can lose yourself in a book –
and that's very different from losing
yourself on the A38 outside Staines.**

Human beings have beguiled the dark with stories,
ever since we invented fire and sat around it.

The book you read can be a voice inside your head,
guiding you, amusing you, reassuring you on life's
tricky path.

Which is why self-help volumes like "If it's Tuesday, it
must be onion soup" are particularly popular.
Although you'll find the same things said, at about a
third of the cost, in the classics section.

That's the thing about bookshops – they're a treasure
trove of amazing stuff, 90% of which you don't even
know about yet.

And there are loads of authors to get to know.

Personally, I was very pleased to see the last Jeffrey Archer book, because I sincerely hope it will be.

But whichever author you're a fan of, time spent reading is time spent enriching your inner life.

Because you can find yourself in a book as well.

> **So what's it worth?**
> You've just booked yourself a thrilling **£53,660**. Yes, you did read that right.

MON	TUES	WED	THURS	FRI
Work	*Work*	*Work*	*Work*	*Work*

SAT

Cinema

SUN

Golf

THE WEEKEND STARTS HERE

Weekends play a massive part in our lives, way beyond the actual
two days.

We look forward to them, and we look back on them.
Disproportionately and delightedly.

It's rather like that scene in one of the lesser-known James Bond
books, "Colonel Sun", which was written by Kingsley Amis. Bond is
being tortured by some baddie using just implements from a kitchen
drawer. And he comes to the conclusion that the feeling of pain
stopping is more blissful than any other sensation, including orgasm.

That's how some weekends are.

But others are about – finding new friends, finding new pubs, finding
new paths across the clifftops of Devon. So, whether yours is a
Christopher-Columbus-style voyage of discovery, or just tucking
yourself under the duvet with some croissants and the funny papers –
enjoy it.

One of the most civilised bits of email banter to have emerged
recently is when people end work-related messages by saying "Enjoy
the weekend". I've often debated with myself when the earliest time of
the week is that you can say that.

And I've decided it's Monday at 9.01 am.

So what's it worth?
It's difficult not to have that
Friday feeling when you discover
it's worth **£49,764**.

IF THE WEATHER'S NICE, GET OUT AND ENJOY IT

The weather makes a *huge* difference to how we feel.

And it may even go some way to explaining the bizarre feelings we have for weather presenters on TV, even though most of them are probably just clothes models who've been given three hours coaching on what an isobar is.

(I reckon if I knew what an isobar was, I'd be able to do that job. I've got some good teeth left, and I can stand up reasonably straight.)

A sunny day means we're smiling at strangers and feeling at one with the world. A torrential downpour means scuffles in the bus queue, particularly in that bit between the bus shelter roof and the inside of the bus, where the rain can sneak down the back of your neck.

And that explains why the Italians have a carefree attitude to life that is sometimes missing in the residents of Helsinki during the nine months of the year when they can't see anything and the ground underneath them freezes into comedy, impossible-to-stand-on ice.

It's all about feeling better. And when the sun shines, everybody feels like a million dollars.

So what's it worth?
Make hay while the sun shines. If you've spent time doing a bit of blue sky thinking recently you can enjoy the summery sum of **£89,625**.

GIVING

······················

As Johnny Carson said, the worst gift is fruitcake. There's only one fruitcake in the entire world, and people keep sending it to each other.

But the old truism is surprisingly true – it's better to give than to receive.

Certainly that was true of one Christmas I spent with my extended family. Someone on my brother's wife's side of the family had wrapped up a small rock for me.

When I feigned delight and asked the obvious question, "Wow – what is it?", she replied that it was a paperweight, and I replied (in time-honoured fashion) that that was exactly what I wanted. I like to think that this rock gave that old woman enormous pleasure as she thought, "Let's see what Steve makes of this." It may even be that she's laughing about it now, regaling chums with the story of the "gift-wrapped rock".

Make no mistake about it, giving is good. I don't know why, it would seem to contradict the laws of nature, but the person who wraps the present seems to get more pure happiness out of the process than the unwrappee.

In other words – the more you give, the richer you feel.

So what's it worth?
Giving gives you
£36,705. Now,
are you going to
keep it or give
that away as well?

ENJOYING GOOD FOOD

Buy good quality food and really enjoy it.

And the longer you spend enjoying each mouthful, the fewer mouthfuls you'll need…

That's the theory, anyway.

So what's it worth? Considering you've just made a very tasty **£58,459**, you can afford to be generous with the tip.

GOING OUT ON THE TOWN WITH YOUR MATES

It's great to go out with friends – although what happens later on in the evening can cause a few problems.

Heineken had a really brave website once where they showed people talking too much, groping, fighting, etc – all the things we've all done after a few too many bevvies.

But if something terrible happens to you, real friends are the people who won't laugh.

Although they might have a hard time keeping a straight face.

Having duly said all that, life should be full of adventure.

As a rock star said once, when asked for his philosophy of life – your life gets a lot richer if you become just a little bit braver than you are right now.

So, go for it. Let your hair down. Tell your mates that they're the best, best, best friends you've ever had.

Explore what the night has to offer.

And remember that you can actually enjoy good times with your friends without getting rat-arsed sometimes.

Women can nod at each other for up to an hour in a coffee shop.

Men just sort of point in the same direction.

So what's it worth?
Doubles all round – you've just accrued **£13,320**.

COOKING

....

An archaeologist from the planet Narda in the 30th century would take one look at our society and think we were obsessed with cooking.

In fact, they might decide that the people who knew the secrets of "braised pork escalopes nestling on a bed of raddiccio" were our gods.

With Jamie Oliver as a sort of cheeky chappy god-next-door.

But cooking is actually very good for us. If you cook your own food, you're less likely to eat the sort of junk which the High Street shoves in our faces.

And men, as well making the fieriest chefs, are now proving that they can do a bit of pan-shaking at home too.

A former colleague of mine set up a blog called "Fire and knives", which is a brilliant way of summing up the appeal of this skill to some men.

So even if you're only capable of boiling a line-caught hen's egg and serving it with mi-cuit Hovis garnished with shavings of Marmite… give it a go.

So what's it worth?
Like the home-made bread in the oven, your riches have just risen by **£31,947**.

GOING ON HOLIDAY

**It's important to approach holidays
in the right spirit.**

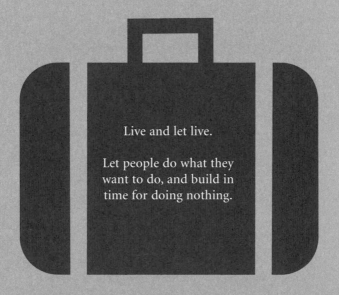

Live and let live.

Let people do what they
want to do, and build in
time for doing nothing.

Otherwise the stress of being on holiday can mean you need another
one when you get back.

Alain de Botton tells the story of a French artist who decided to
travel to England, got as far as a pub near the Gare du Nord, and
decided after a few hours there that he'd seen enough of English
culture and went straight home again.

In fact, there are some philosophers who question the value of holidays at all – saying that we take our personalities and problems with us, so why should anything change just because the sun is shining and the palm tree is nice and bendy?

But speaking personally, I've always found that bright sunshine and a bendy palm tree can put most other things into perspective rather nicely.

So what's it worth?
A change is as good as a holiday, but if you've taken a holiday in the past few months that's worth **£91,750** of happiness. And that's a lot of change.

BEING IN A STABLE RELATIONSHIP

What defines a great relationship?

Well, if you look at nature you can learn some interesting things.

For instance, chimpanzees in the wild live in a violent, intensely competitive society. However, their close relatives the bonobos live in a society which is relatively peaceful.

As Hannah Holmes, a global expert on primate behaviour, has written – bonobos "rarely encounter a conflict they can't resolve by copulating".

So there you have it.

And don't knock it. If it works for monkeys…

In fact, I think we all know people in relationships like that.

Maybe that helps to explain the scientific evidence about people living longer if they're in a relationship.

I almost said "stable relationship" just then, but after all the nature stuff earlier, you might think I meant living with a horse.

So what's it worth?
Happiness is clearly better shared. If you're in a relationship you can bank on having someone there to make you a cup of tea in the morning and you can also bank **£154,849**.

THE SENSE OF CAMARADERIE AT WORK

Do you know why freelancers always meet each other in Starbucks? Because the one, solid-gold, guaranteed good thing about having a job is the sociable side of it.

And freelancers miss that.

Gathering around the water cooler or the kettle for a good old natter.

Temps miss it too. Unless they're spectacularly good-looking, in which case they may get too much of it.

Something I heard recently bore all this out rather beautifully, I thought.

There's an ad agency where the employees voted for pay cuts rather than job losses.

They liked each other more than money.

I love that.

Mind you, that kind of team-spirit is quite rare in ad agencies.

(Which is rather like saying "That story about a shark carrying a drowning man on his back for 30 miles is a bit unusual, isn't it?")

So what's it worth?
A pay rise of **£37,229**.
It certainly works for us.

ENJOYING YOUR FAVOURITE DRINK

If it's a triple Baileys and vodka, you might have to go easy on it.

There are a lot of people who become over-fond of alcohol with the word "super" or "extra" in the name, and it can be great fun talking to them, but quite often I find I don't have the right change.

However, there's a whole range of stuff to tantalise your taste buds – from a well-balanced glass of Merlot to a well-made cup of espresso.

For some people, a pot of tea absolutely hits the spot.

And here's a tip. If you like something sweet in the evening, try one of those low-calorie hot chocolate drinks.

And whoever said "a hot drink at bedtime is just a substitute for hot sex" – all right goddamit, you're right.

So what's it worth?
If you've ordered your drink of choice of late add **£29,651** to the tab.

HAVING CHILDREN

I've got two kids, and I have to tell you that their every breath fills my life with sunshine and the sound of angels singing.

I have to tell you that, or they'll make my life hell.

I remember when my first child was born and I held her in my arms for the first time.

I blubbed like a baby myself.

She probably took one look at me and thought, "Who's this drama queen? I'm the one who's just been through hell on earth, and Mum over there hasn't been having a picnic, but your man here has just been standing around."

(I don't know why my eldest daughter was born with an Irish accent, it's just one of those things.)

And the truth of the matter is, I was crying so hard because I knew how much money she was going to cost me over the coming years.

But seriously.

Kids are absolutely priceless.

If you've got them, you'll know that.

And, if you haven't… enjoy the lie-in.

£123,592

So what's it worth?
No wonder large families are always happy, you receive
£123,592 worth of happiness for each child. More than
enough to look after you well into retirement.

LEARNING SOMETHING NEW

This is part of the appeal of programmes like "Mastermind". So that we can all be the owners of information like the fact that the elephant is the only mammal which cannot jump.

Completely useless information.

But it gives us a nice glow.

And then there are useful things we can learn too. Like basic plumbing, basic car maintenance, or – the evening class I'm going to do – "basically, what's the difference between a spanner and a screwdriver?"

You can learn a foreign language. And bear in mind that one of the top comedians on TV has said that there are only two things in life which are unfailingly funny – "people hurting themselves and foreign accents".

So watching a foreigner hit their thumb with a hammer in the "Brazilian DIY Beginners Class" should be a guaranteed side-splitter.

These days, the courses are getting more exotic too. You can sign up for non-contact martial arts programmes (in which you stare the other person to death).

> **So what's it worth?**
> Bet you didn't know that if you learnt something new recently, you earned the equivalent of **£60,171**. Now you do.

YOUR BIRTHDAY

You know that feeling you have when it's your birthday and you're maybe 9 years old?

You think to yourself – "Well, everything has to go right today. It's my birthday, so everybody has to be nice to me, and all the nice things need to happen, and every second of today is going to be special, because this is my day."

It's a really good feeling.

In fact, it's such a good feeling, it seems a waste to limit it to just one day of the year.

So what's it worth?
Unless you were born on February 29th, this is an automatic **£35,542**. Enjoy it.

LOOKING GOOD

There's a thin line between feeling good about how you look, and pure, vacuous vanity.

And, ironically, there is nothing we find less attractive than vanity.

If we start going out with somebody and they spend forever looking in the mirror – well, that's about as big a put-off as you can get.

(Short of getting violently drunk and declaring to your date, "I fancy you. You remind me of my mother.")

But taking pride in how you look is a good thing.

Although we can learn something useful from kids here. Sometimes kids want to dress UP. Sometimes they want to dress DOWN. And usually they look great either way.

I think the reason is that they're doing what they want to do.

It's all about feeling good about how you look – which frankly matters a whole lot more than how you do look.

> **So what's it worth?**
> You should be pleased with your figure. Particularly when it's **£37,575**.

Incidentally, nice clothes needn't be expensive. You can get some amazing stuff in those charity shops in the High Street. Although they sometimes remind me of that film *Dead Man Walking*. Or the follow-up, *Dead Man Scratching his Bollocks*.

BEING TOLD "I LOVE YOU"

A famous comedian once said that "love" was the only four-letter word he didn't use during sex.

And I think that tells us all we need to know about his sex life.

Because "I love you" are probably the three nicest words you can ever hear. Particularly during sex.

The 3 worst words would probably be "Shift your arse" or "Mind my bike".

Or "Who are you?"

Or "Was that it?"

Conventional wisdom has it that you should never say "I love you" unless you mean it. But I disagree.

People will feel better hearing it, so say it as often as you can. Personally, I like to go one-up on the bank tellers who wish me a nice day, as follows…

Me – "Can I pay in this cheque please?"

Them – "Certainly, sir. Is there anything else we can do for you today?"

Me – "I love you."

(Pause.)

Them – "Have a nice day."

So what's it worth?
Money can't buy you love but hearing the words "I Love You" is worth **£164,921**.

LAUGHING

Here's one.
....

This blonde rings the fire brigade and says, "My flat is on fire, please come straightaway." "Certainly," replies the fireman. "What's the quickest way to get there?"

She says: "Hullo? In the big red engine?"

Here's another one.

My dad worked as a bin-man and I used to hate it when he came to pick me up from school. Not because of the shame, it was just that I never knew exactly which day he was going to come.

Maybe those gags tickle your humerus, or maybe they don't. But it's been proved again and again that laughing is very good for you. Some people have cured themselves of life-threatening diseases by watching funny DVDs for weeks on end. (That's true.)

What's funny?

Well, I like Mel Brooks' quote. "Comedy," he said, "is when you fall down and break your leg. Tragedy is when I have a slight cold."

Some people seem to find everything funny. They're the luckiest people alive.

And they're much prized in the studio audience for "Two Pints of Lager and a Packet of Crisps".

So what's it worth?
If you've enjoyed a grin, a giggle or a guffaw over the past few months, you are laughing all the way to the bank. Collect **£108,021**.

HAVING GOOD HEALTH

I went to the doctor and said, "I've got this strawberry stuck up my bum," and he said, "Don't worry, I've got some cream for that."

This other bloke was in there and he had fried eggs all over his shirt, baked beans in his hair, and a sausage jammed in each ear. I said, "What's wrong with you?" He said, "Oh it's nothing serious, I'm just not eating properly."

We tend to use jokes to defuse things we're afraid of, and ill health is one of the biggest things we all fear.

But for 95% of your life, you'll probably be fit as a flea playing a fiddle.

So enjoy that.

And just be thankful that you're very unlikely to suffer from Cotard's Syndrome. That's a real disease, in which the sufferer believes that they're dead.

"Good morning. How are you today, Mr Jones?"

"Not so good, doctor. I passed away last night."

So what's it worth?
If you're in good health, be happy, it's worth **£180,589**.

MORNINGS

Mondays are a terrible way to spend one-seventh of your life, aren't they?

And actually we do tend to have predictable highs and lows during a week.

Monday mornings tend to be horrible, Friday afternoons tend to be lovely.

But what's also predictable is that every day has its sunrise.

Every day has a morning.

And that morning can bring with it a huge sense of promise and change.

Today, everything could be better.

Today, everything could be fantastic.

Believe it, and it just might happen.

If this rampant optimism gets you down, remember the words of one American comedian. He said, "People tell me it takes more energy to frown than to smile. I tell them it takes more energy to point that out than to leave me alone."

So what's it worth?
The early bird catches **£17,652**. That's got to be worth getting up for.

Every day has its sunset – and sunsets tend to be the most beautiful part of any day.

If you don't agree, I hope you never get a job on the board of a company selling postcards. You'll get into more arguments than you ever believed possible.

So make the most of sunsets, and don't stay in the office when the show is starting.

Some people love evenings because they bring a sense of completion, a chance to look back at all you've achieved during the day and give yourself a pat on the back.

Others, because that's when the pubs start to liven up.

★

★

★

So what's it worth?
You might want to make a night of it, you've just banked **£45,328**.

LIFE IN THE CITY

**Samuel Johnson famously said that a man
who is tired of London is tired of life.**

History doesn't record what he had to say about Croydon
town centre.

Richard Burton (the writer, not the actor) spent years writing a huge
book called *The Anatomy of Melancholy*. After a lifetime's study, he
came to a conclusion as to what was the best thing to do if you
suffered from this.

And the answer was simple – keep busy.

And that's what cities can do for you.

Just look at what you can do, any night of the week, in London. Virtually anything you can imagine doing, plus about 70 things you'd never think of. Of course, the people who live in London don't do any of that – the theatres and ballets are full of tourists and people who come in from the suburbs for the evening.

But that's not the point.

So what's it worth?
Bright lights, big figures. An urban lifestyle is worth an urbane **£11,185**.

SUPPORTING YOUR FAVOURITE TEAM

The thing about supporting a team is that it's an addiction.

A friend of mine once explained the appeal of smoking like this. "To a smoker, if they lose their job, or their partner walks out, or their house burns down – they've still got that little packet in their pocket or handbag. It's reassurance."

(This is analysis, by the way, not encouragement.)

And it's the same with supporting, whether it's football or the local ladies' badminton team.

Although generally speaking, it's a lot healthier than smoking a packet of Craven untipped.

It doesn't matter what else happens in your world – wars might be declared, earthquakes might happen – but Hartlepool are going to lose.

It's a certainty.

In fact, last week the police were asked to investigate the Football League, because there was a suspicion of betting irregularities.

Apparently, someone had put a tenner on Hartlepool to win.

And although it's a bit of a risk taking a young kid along to a football match – because there's something quite unnerving about seeing a 7-year-old stand there in his brand new scarf and bobble hat while 2 feet away a man screams obscenities you've never heard into his left ear – well, it's a bonding exercise, isn't it?

And a learning experience.

I learned never to take my kids to my local club until they were old enough to swear back.

So what's it worth?
Don't worry whether your team has won or lost. Supporting them is supporting you to the value of **£29,100**.

EATING CHOCOLATE

Remember what it was like to lick the chocolate from the baking bowl?

And it's not just kids who love chocolate, obviously.

We all do.

Chocolate releases the same chemicals that are released during orgasm.

And with chocolate, you don't have to wake up next to someone the next day and say, "Excuse me, do I live here, or do you?"

In fact, if they invented a chocolate bar that could put up a set of shelves, I think most blokes would be out on their ear.

So what's it worth?
It may cost as little as 60p but it's worth **£40,808**. If you've enjoyed a piece lately, you get a piece of that.

DOING SOMEONE A FAVOUR

You know that feeling you get when you hear a bee buzzing against a window pane, and you pluck up the courage to go over and open the window?

And then the bee flies free.

You feel really good, don't you?

Partly because you were fantastically brave going near such a dangerous wild beast.

Partly because the noise was driving you crazy.

But also because you did another creature a favour.

It's the same if you hand in a wallet.

(Funnily enough, especially if it belongs to a bee.)

Sure, that £45 could have come in handy – in fact, come to think of it, maybe that was my wallet, because I'm sure I had £45 and someone else's credit cards in there. But in truth, you feel so much better if you do someone else a favour.

The great thinker Edward de Bono tells this story, to illustrate the point.

A famous king had a beautiful daughter – and two princes who were trying to win her hand. One of them did everything he could for the king (washed his chariot, fixed the squeaky bit on the drawbridge, etc). The other one asked the king to lend him his chariot because he needed it to visit his sick mother.

The second one won – because the king felt so much better doing him a favour, than he did with the other prince.

It might sound like complicated psychological stuff – but actually it's a universal truth.

Doing someone a favour will make you feel great.

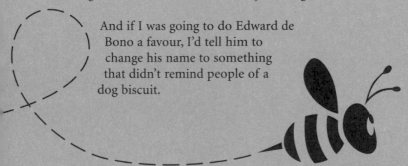

And if I was going to do Edward de Bono a favour, I'd tell him to change his name to something that didn't remind people of a dog biscuit.

So what's it worth?
It's better to give than receive. Do yourself a favour, take **£57,010** for your good deeds.

PERFORMING MUSIC

In the mid-1970s, a revolution took place in the British music scene.

A magazine called *Sideburns* printed diagrams showing how to play three basic chords on a guitar. "Now," it said, "form a band."

Thus was born the Punk Era, in which people who couldn't even manage two and a half of those chords became world-famous as musicians just by changing their name to "Norman Knob".

But the magazine, and the movement, had a serious purpose.

To encourage more people to play music.

Because there is very little that is more satisfying than picking up a guitar and trying to master the opening to "Smells Like Teen Spirit".

It's just the poor sod next door I feel sorry for.

So what's it worth?
Picking up an instrument picks up your wealth to the tune of **£30,008**. Far be it from us to suggest you spend it on some lessons…

THE REALLY RICH LIST

1.	HAVING GOOD HEALTH:	GBP 180,589
2.	BEING TOLD "I LOVE YOU":	GBP 164,921
3.	BEING IN A STABLE RELATIONSHIP:	GBP 154,849
4.	LIVING IN A PEACEFUL AND SAFE COUNTRY:	GBP 129,448
5.	HAVING CHILDREN:	GBP 123,592
6.	SPENDING TIME WITH YOUR FAMILY:	GBP 110,047
7.	LAUGHING:	GBP 108,021
8.	HAVING SEX:	GBP 105,210
9.	GOING ON HOLIDAY:	GBP 91,759
10.	SAVOURING THE PEACE AND QUIET:	GBP 89,828
11.	IF THE WEATHER'S NICE GET OUT AND ENJOY IT:	GBP 89,625
12.	BEING IN THE COUNTRYSIDE:	GBP 88,077
13.	HAVING TIME TO YOURSELF:	GBP 80,558
14.	REFLECTING ON HAPPY MEMORIES:	GBP 80,419
15.	PETS:	GBP 78,640
16.	THE GREAT OUTDOORS:	GBP 74,310
17.	A JOB WELL DONE:	GBP 70,676
18.	TAKE UP A HOBBY:	GBP 70,041
19.	LISTENING TO MUSIC:	GBP 68,823
20.	SPENDING TIME WITH FRIENDS:	GBP 63,256
21.	FEELING AT HOME:	GBP 62,963
22.	LEARNING SOMETHING NEW:	GBP 60,171
23.	ENJOYING GOOD FOOD:	GBP 58,459
24.	YOU'RE CREATIVE:	GBP 57,075
25.	DOING SOMEONE A FAVOUR:	GBP 57,010

26. **TAKING A DAY OFF:**	GBP 54,428
27. **LITERATURE:**	GBP 53,660
28. **THE WEEKEND STARTS HERE:**	GBP 49,764
29. **DOING THINGS ON THE SPUR OF THE MOMENT:**	GBP 47,528
30. **A WALK IN THE PARK:**	GBP 47,007
31. **EVENINGS:**	GBP 45,328
32. **CONTEMPLATING BEAUTIFUL THINGS:**	GBP 41,716
33. **EATING CHOCOLATE:**	GBP 40,808
34. **LOOKING GOOD:**	GBP 37,575
35. **THE SENSE OF CAMARADERIE AT WORK:**	GBP 37,229
36. **FEEL BETTER, FEEL FITTER:**	GBP 36,970
37. **GIVING:**	GBP 36,705
38. **FAITH:**	GBP 36,530
39. **YOUR BIRTHDAY:**	GBP 34,542
40. **KNOWING YOUR NEIGHBOURS:**	GBP 33,698
41. **BEING PART OF THE COMMUNITY:**	GBP 33,665
42. **COOKING:**	GBP 31,947
43. **PERFORMING MUSIC:**	GBP 30,008
44. **ENJOYING YOUR FAVOURITE DRINK:**	GBP 29,651
45. **SUPPORTING YOUR FAVOURITE TEAM:**	GBP 29,100
46. **PLAYING TEAM GAMES:**	GBP 23,475
47. **GOING OUT TO THE FLICKS:**	GBP 21,615
48. **MORNINGS:**	GBP 17,652
49. **GOING OUT ON THE TOWN WITH YOUR MATES:**	GBP 13,320
50. **LIFE IN THE CITY:**	GBP 11,185

FIVE THINGS WE LEARNT FROM ASKING 1,000 PEOPLE QUESTIONS

1. We're now 100% positive that positive thoughts make for positive people

It seems that the media's recession obsession is literally and figuratively driving everybody to depression.

On the other hand, when our researchers asked people to think about what made them happy, it made them happy.

2. By putting a value on what we value we appreciate the value of what we value

Compare the amounts given to spending time with your family (£110,047), compared to getting drunk (£13,320). Or being in the countryside (£88,077) as opposed to being in the city (£11,185).

It makes you think how we "invest" rather than "spend" our time.

3. Just "be" it

Just look at the difference between the topics towards the top of the table:

Being with friends, being in love, being healthy, being in a relationship, being with nature .

… and those towards the bottom…

Getting drunk, getting up, going to the cinema, going out.

Maybe that's why we are called Human Beings rather than Human Doings.

4. The more it costs the less it's worth

You don't have to be rich to be really rich. Only one out of the top ten (going on holiday) involves going to the bank.

5. Happiness is a lot closer than you think

Sit down and look around you. There's a very good chance that from where you are now you're worth a lot more than you might have originally thought.

A NOTE ON THE RESEARCH
....

At the intersection of economics, sociology, and psychology, there's a wealth of academic study on the relationship between life events – like illness, marriage, or unemployment – and their effects on human happiness. These studies use mathematical models to estimate the size and impact of these relationships expressed in monetary terms. For example, a 2007 study by Nattavudh Powdthavee of York University found that an increase in the frequency of interaction with friends, relatives and neighbours is worth up to an extra £85,000 a year in terms of life satisfaction, whereas actual changes in income themselves buy very little happiness.

These studies are complicated affairs. They require large amounts of data, culled from the same people taking the same survey every year, over several years. But we were inspired by them and, working with the research specialists BrainJuicer, used them as the starting point in developing our own method. Our aim was to create a survey that was easy to understand, fun and simple to take, and capable of delivering accurate findings.

We spoke to a nationally representative sample of 1,000 people. We asked them how happy each of the fifty different life events and experiences would make them, and to rate them on a happiness scale of 1 to 10. As well as these fifty variables, we also asked people to rate five additional variables of monetary value, expressed in terms of lottery wins.

The levels of happiness expected from these lottery wins allowed us to estimate the value of the other life events and experiences.

For example, if the average expected happiness rating from a £100,000 lottery win was five, and an individual respondent rated having sex also as five, we said that for that individual having sex brings the same level of happiness as they'd expect from a £100,000 lottery win. We repeated this process for each individual respondent, before averaging these values to arrive at our final figure – in this case, in terms of happiness, having sex is the worth the equivalent of £105,210.

No method is without its shortcomings, and one of the most common difficulties in asking people questions about how happy they expect certain events or experiences to make them is the "focussing illusion", a cognitive bias that means when we contemplate any major life change, we tend to overestimate the effect it will have. Taking this into account, it was interesting to note that many people we spoke to believed money would bring diminishing returns of happiness. Much of our sample expected different lottery wins to bring the same level of happiness – they judged there to be no difference in the effect of winning a million compared to winning ten million, and gave them both the same rating on the happiness scale. In these instances, we assumed the larger lottery win to be worth the same as the smaller lottery win.

In comparison to the scholarly work, our method may not be as watertight and our findings may not be as accurate. But our intention differs from theirs. While the academics are interested in advising on public policy, we're interested in beginning a public conversation. A conversation on the value of those everyday pleasures that are available to all, irrespective of wealth, and that we sometimes take for granted. I hope you find the results as interesting as it has been to collect them.

Matt Boffey, April 2009

REALLY RICH BY... AGE

TOP 10, AGE 18 - 34

1. Being told "I love you":   GBP 186,971

2. Being in a stable relationship: GBP 163,661

3. Having good health: GBP 153,361

4. Having children: GBP 120,887

5. Having sex: GBP 111,037

6. Laughing: GBP 106,213

7. Living in a peaceful and safe country: GBP 94,544

8. Going on holiday: GBP 87,152

9. Spending time with your family: GBP 82,954

10. Savouring the peace and quiet: GBP 76,773

Lowest ranking – Mornings: GBP 4,949

TOP 10, AGE 35+

1. Having good health: GBP 197,707

2. Living in a peaceful and safe country: GBP 151,391

3. Being told "I love you":   GBP 151,058

4. Being in a stable relationship: GBP 149,309

5. Spending time with your family: GBP 127,080

6. Having children: GBP 125,298

7. Laughing: GBP 109,158

8. Having sex: GBP 101,546

9. If the weather's nice, get out and enjoy it: GBP 100,535

10. Savouring the peace and quiet: GBP 98,036

Lowest ranking – Getting drunk: GBP 9,415

REALLY RICH BY... LOCATION

TOP 10, THE NORTH

1. Being told "I love you": GBP 178,560

2. Having good health: GBP 169,786

3. Being in a stable relationship: GBP 169,674

4. Living in a peaceful and safe country: GBP 147,192

5. Having children: GBP 145,274

6. Spending time with your family: GBP 124,555

7. Laughing: GBP 110,236

8. Having sex: GBP 106,606

9. Being in the countryside: GBP 95,332

10. Going on holiday: GBP 92,271

Lowest ranking - Life in the city: GBP 6,477

TOP 10, THE SOUTH

1. Having good health: GBP 178,672

2. Being told "I love you": GBP 166,037

3. Being in a stable relationship: GBP 136,446

4. Having sex: GBP 123,956

5. Living in a peaceful and safe country: GBP 112,209

6. Laughing: GBP 107,800

7. Spending time with your family: GBP 107,800

8. Having children: GBP 104,913

9. If the weather's nice, get out and enjoy it: GBP 101,788

10. Pets: GBP 97,807

Lowest ranking - Life in the city: GBP 6,477

REALLY RICH BY... GENDER

TOP 10, MALE

1. Having good health: GBP 181,105

2. Being told "I love you": GBP 163,424

3. Being in a stable relationship: GBP 160,770

4. Having sex: GBP 137,909

5. Living in a peaceful and safe country: GBP 132,989

6. Being in the countryside: GBP 105,114

7. Savouring the peace and quiet: GBP 101,665

8. Laughing: GBP 100,717

9. If the weather's nice, get out and enjoy it: GBP 99,195

10. Spending time with your family: GBP 95,443

Lowest ranking - Life in the city: GBP 6,477

TOP 10, FEMALE

1. Having good health: GBP 180,089

2. Being told "I love you": GBP 166,371

3. Having children: GBP 154,624

4. Being in a stable relationship: GBP 149,110

5. Living in a peaceful and safe country: GBP 126,015

6. Spending time with family: GBP 124,201

7. Laughing: GBP 115,099

8. Going on holiday: GBP 91,871

9. Pets: GBP 91,641

10. Reflecting on happy memories: GBP 87,620

Lowest ranking - Playing sport: GBP 7,565

HOW REALLY RICH ARE YOU?

By adding together the totals for every topic that is relevant to you, you can quickly work out how really rich you are.

	ACTIVITY	VALUE	CHECK	SCORE
1.	Having good health:	GBP 180,589	☐	
2.	Being told "I love you":	GBP 164,921	☐	
3.	Being in a stable relationship:	GBP 154,849	☐	
4.	Living in a peaceful and safe country:	GBP 129,448	☐	
5.	Having children:	GBP 123,592	☐	
6.	Spending time with your family:	GBP 110,047	☐	
7.	Laughing:	GBP 108,021	☐	
8.	Having sex:	GBP 105,210	☐	
9.	Going on holiday:	GBP 91,759	☐	
10.	Savouring the peace and quiet:	GBP 89,828	☐	
11.	If the weather's nice, get out and enjoy it:	GBP 89,625	☐	
12.	Being in the countryside:	GBP 88,077	☐	
13.	Having time to yourself:	GBP 80,558	☐	
14.	Reflecting on happy memories:	GBP 80,419	☐	
15.	Pets:	GBP 78,640	☐	
16.	The great outdoors:	GBP 74,310	☐	
17.	A job well done:	GBP 70,676	☐	
18.	Take up a hobby:	GBP 70,041	☐	
19.	Listening to music:	GBP 68,823	☐	
20.	Spending time with friends:	GBP 63,256	☐	
21.	Being at home:	GBP 62,963	☐	
22.	Learning something new:	GBP 60,171	☐	
23.	Enjoying good food:	GBP 58,459	☐	
24.	You're creative:	GBP 57,075	☐	
25.	Doing someone a favour:	GBP 57,010	☐	

	ACTIVITY	VALUE	CHECK	SCORE
26.	Taking a day off:	GBP 54,428	☐	
27.	Literature:	GBP 53,660	☐	
28.	The weekend starts here:	GBP 49,764	☐	
29.	Doing things on the spur of the moment:	GBP 47,528	☐	
30.	A walk in the park:	GBP 47,007	☐	
31.	Evenings:	GBP 45,328	☐	
32.	Contemplating beautiful things:	GBP 41,716	☐	
33.	Eating chocolate:	GBP 40,808	☐	
34.	Looking good:	GBP 37,575	☐	
35.	The sense of camaraderie at work:	GBP 37,229	☐	
36.	Feel better, feel fitter:	GBP 36,970	☐	
37.	Giving:	GBP 36,705	☐	
38.	Faith:	GBP 36,530	☐	
39.	Your birthday:	GBP 34,542	☐	
40.	Knowing your neighbours:	GBP 33,698	☐	
41.	Being part of the community:	GBP 33,665	☐	
42.	Cooking:	GBP 31,947	☐	
43.	Performing music:	GBP 30,008	☐	
44.	Enjoying your favourite drink:	GBP 29,651	☐	
45.	Supporting your favourite team:	GBP 29,100	☐	
46.	Playing team games:	GBP 23,475	☐	
47.	Going out to the flicks:	GBP 21,615	☐	
48.	Mornings:	GBP 17,652	☐	
49.	Going out on the town with your mates:	GBP 13,320	☐	
50.	Life in the city:	GBP 11,185	☐	

TOTAL

If you would like to get a more accurate calculation go to **www.reallyrichlist.com** Here you can take the original survey, calculate exactly how much you are really worth, and find out where you sit on the Really Rich List.